D1243877

(11-10-04)   G
18.95

D

Discovering Antarctica

The Future

June Loves

CHELSEA HOUSE
PUBLISHERS

A Haights Cross Communications Company

Philadelphia

This edition first published in 2003 in the United States of America by Chelsea House Publishers, a subsidiary of Haights Cross Communications.

Chelsea House Publishers
1974 Sproul Road, Suite 400
Broomall, PA 19008-0914

The Chelsea House world wide web address is www.chelseahouse.com

Library of Congress Cataloging-in-Publication Data
Loves, June.
    Discovering Antarctica. The future / by June Loves.
    p. cm. — (Discovering Antarctica)
    Summary: Describes the discovery and exploration of Antarctica, territorial claims, treaties, tourism, and global scientific cooperation in terms of the future.
    ISBN 0-7910-7025-5
    1. Antarctica—Discovery and exploration—Juvenile literature. 2. Antarctica—Research—Juvenile literature. 3. Antarctica—International status—Juvenile literature. [1. Antarctica.] I. Title. II. Series.
    G863 .L678 2003
    919.8'904—dc21

                                                                    2002001415

First published 1998 by
MACMILLAN EDUCATION AUSTRALIA PTY LTD
627 Chapel Street, South Yarra, Australia, 3141

Copyright © June Loves 1998
Copyright in photographs © individual photographers as credited
Illustrations copyright © Margaret Hastie 1998
Designed by Andrea Jaretzki
Cover design by Dimitrios Frangoulis
Typeset by Polar Design

Printed in China

Acknowledgements
The author would like to thank Rod Seppelt and Maria Turnbull of the Australian Antarctic Division for their assistance.

Cover: Galen Rowell/Hedgehog House/AUSCAPE

AUSCAPE International, p. 14 (left); Gary Ball/Hedgehog House, NZ/AUSCAPE, p. 5 (top); Coo-ee Picture Library, pp. 6, 7, 20 (top); Paul Ensor, Hedgehog House, NZ/AUSCAPE, p. 15 (top); Jean-Paul Ferrero/AUSCAPE, pp. 17, 29 (bottom), 29; Great Southern Stock, pp. 22 (right) © Trezise, 28 (top) © Mike Pole; International Photographic Library, pp. 14 (right), 20 (left); P. Leroux-Explorer/AUSCAPE, p. 18 (bottom); JA McDonald/Antarctica NZ/Hedgehog House NZ/AUSCAPE, p. 16 (bottom); D. Parer & E. Parer-Cook/AUSCAPE, pp. 13 (top), 27 (left); Rod Ledingham, pp. 11, 12, 24, 25 (bottom), 27 (bottom) © R. Besso; C. Monteath/AUSCAPE, pp. 5 (bottom), 10, 13 (bottom), 22 (top), 23, 25 (top); Skip Novak, Hedgehog House, NZ/AUSCAPE, p. 18 & 19; Chris Rudge, Hedgehog House, NZ/AUSCAPE, pp. 16 (top), 26; Dick Smith/Hedgehog House, NZ/AUSCAPE, p. 9 (bottom); Kim Westerskov, Hedgehog House, NZ/AUSCAPE, p. 19 (right).

Words that appear in **bold type** can be found in the Glossary on page 31.

Contents

Introduction

Antarctica is the fifth largest continent in the world. Most of Antarctica is covered in snow and ice throughout the year. Fierce storms and extreme cold are all part of life in the Antarctic region.

▶ Human activities such as tourism need to be carefully controlled to protect the Antarctic environment and wildlife.

▼ As people from different nations work together, it is hoped that the Antarctic environment can be studied and protected for the benefit of all the world.

The Importance of Antarctica

Antarctica's **remote** position in the world and harsh climate have made it the last continent to be explored and developed by humans. Today, human activities such as tourism, fishing, scientific research, and the development and maintenance of research bases, all pose a potential threat to the environment. Successful management is needed to protect and **conserve** Antarctica for the future.

Most nations of the world recognize the value of Antarctica's frozen wilderness and the importance of the knowledge that can be gained there.

Discovery and Exploration

Since the time of the ancient Greeks, people had suspected that a large continent existed at the bottom of the world. However, Antarctica still was only a **myth** until 200 years ago.

Captain James Cook was the first to sail near the coast of Antarctica in 1772–75. He never actually saw the continent, but he and his crew were the first to cross the **Antarctic Circle**, sailing farther south than anyone before them.

▲ Early explorers had to cope with the freezing temperatures, poor food, and isolation of the Antarctic.

◀ Many ships became trapped in ice while trying to explore the Antarctic continent. Some ships were trapped for up to a year before being rescued.

Modern Antarctic Exploration

The invention of aircraft and modern communications has made it easier, quicker, and safer to explore Antarctica.

Early Antarctic Discoveries

Whalers and seal hunters were among the first people to discover Antarctica. In the years to come, brave and courageous explorers **endured** the freezing weather, poor **rations**, and **isolation** to explore mainland Antarctica. Many explorers lost their lives in attempts to uncover the secrets of the Antarctic. Others survived harsh winters, trapped by the ice, until rescuers could reach them.

➤ Captain Robert Scott, the famous Antarctic explorer, lost his life in the harsh Antarctic conditions after traveling to the **South Pole**.

Territorial Claims

Prior to World War II, seven nations had claimed parts of Antarctica for their own. Argentina, Australia, Chile, France, New Zealand, Norway, and the United Kingdom had all made a **claim**, although the claims were not equal. Australia had the largest claim, with 42 percent of the land. The claims of Argentina, the United Kingdom, and Chile all overlapped. One-sixth of Antarctica was still unclaimed.

The United States and Russia did not recognize the claims of the other nations. They believed they could **stake** claims of their own if they decided to do so.

In 1959, all **territorial** claims were **suspended**.

The International Geophysical Year

The International Geophysical Year began in July 1957 and ended in December 1958. It was a great cooperative effort by scientists of the world to study Earth and its environment.

◀ During the International Geophysical Year, the United States established five Antarctic stations, including Amundsen-Scott at the South Pole.

▼ In 1957, Russia set up Vostok station at the Pole of Inaccessibility, the point in Antarctica farthest from all coasts.

A large amount of fieldwork was carried out in Antarctica.

Twelve nations set up more than 50 scientific stations with scientists and support staff to carry out research. The research had a special emphasis on **meteorology**, **oceanography**, and **geomagnetism** in Antarctica.

◀ In the future, Antarctica could become a center of political trouble. At the moment, however, through scientific cooperation between nations, Antarctica is a continent of peace.

The Antarctic Treaty

The International Geophysical Year was very successful in Antarctica.

When it ended, the twelve nations decided to continue their research and scientific cooperation. This led the way for the Antarctic Treaty.

Signing the Antarctic Treaty

Representatives of the twelve nations came together to discuss the future of Antarctica. They proceeded to draw up and sign the Antarctic Treaty, which came into force in June 1961.

▼ The Antarctic Treaty plays an important part in protecting and conserving the plant and animal life, natural resources, and general environment of Antarctica.

Some Antarctic Treaty Rules

- Antarctica should be used only for peaceful purposes.
- Nuclear explosions, the disposal of nuclear waste, and any military activities are banned.
- Freedom of access is permitted to all parts of the continent.
- Freedom of scientific research is guaranteed.

Consultative Members

Forty-four nations have now signed the Antarctic Treaty. Twenty-seven nations are consultative members. This means that these nations must do considerable research in Antarctica. Consultative members meet every two years to review the management of Antarctica.

Nations That Have Signed the Antarctic Treaty (2000)

Nation	Year Signed			Nation	Year Signed	
Belgium	1960	CM	•	Papua New Guinea	1981	
France	1960	CM	•	Peru	1981	CM
Japan	1960	CM	•	Spain	1982	CM
New Zealand	1960	CM	•	China	1983	CM
Norway	1960	CM	•	India	1983	CM
Russian Federation	1960	CM	•	Cuba	1984	
South Africa	1960	CM	•	Finland	1984	CM
United Kingdom	1960	CM	•	Hungary	1984	
United States	1960	CM	•	Sweden	1984	CM
Argentina	1961	CM	•	Republic of Korea	1986	CM
Australia	1961	CM	•	Austria	1987	
Chile	1961	CM	•	DPR of Korea	1987	
Poland	1961	CM		Ecuador	1987	CM
Czech Republic	1962			Greece	1987	
Slovak Republic	1962			Canada	1988	
Denmark	1965			Colombia	1989	
Netherlands	1967	CM		Switzerland	1990	
Romania	1971			Guatemala	1991	
Brazil	1975	CM		Ukraine	1992	
Bulgaria	1978	CM		Turkey	1996	
Germany	1979	CM		Venezuela	1999	
Uruguay	1980	CM				
Italy	1981	CM				

• = Nations that originally signed the Treaty

CM = Consultative Member

▶ Cooperation among the different nations represented in Antarctica is an important part of the Antarctic Treaty.

Conservation of Living Resources

Under the Antarctic Treaty, important conservation agreements have been made to protect Antarctica's living resources and environment.

Conservation of Flora and Fauna

The first conservation agreement was *Agreed Measures for the Conservation of Flora and Fauna (1964)*. It provides general protection for native animals and plants.

Conservation of Seals

In the past, two types of Antarctic seals, the Antarctic fur seal and the southern elephant seal, were hunted close to **extinction**. Beginning in the nineteenth century, the sealing industry hunted seals for their fur and oil. Nearly three million Antarctic fur seals were killed. After the Antarctic fur seal population had been nearly wiped out, hunters turned to southern elephant seals, which were valuable for their oil. It is estimated that more than one million southern elephant seals were killed.

In most areas of Antarctica, commercial sealing finally ended in 1912, and some time later on the **sub-Antarctic island** of South Georgia.

◀ Native birdlife as well as plant and animal life are protected under the Antarctic Treaty.

Convention for Conservation of Antarctic Seals (1978)

The *Convention for Conservation of Antarctic Seals (1978)* protects the seals that remain in Antarctica today. It sets very low limits on the number of seals that can be caught for some groups of seals, and puts a complete ban on hunting others if commercial sealing is ever **resumed**.

More than one million southern elephant seals were killed by sealers for their oil. Today they are protected by an international convention.

Antarctic fur seals were killed in large numbers until commercial sealing was stopped. Today they are a protected **species**.

Conservation of Whales

The International Whaling Commission (IWC) **regulates** whaling in all the oceans around the world. The Antarctic Treaty does not regulate Antarctic whaling.

In the past, Antarctic whales such as humpback, blue, fin, sei, and minke whales, have been hunted to near extinction. Once numbers of one type of whale dropped, another type of whale was hunted until its numbers decreased.

The International Whaling Commission tried to control the number of whales being killed. They limited the times during the year in which whales could be hunted. They also set a minimum size for the whales that could be hunted, to stop young whales from being killed. However, little was known about the **ecology** of whales. No clear scientific limits were set to stop **exploitation**.

➤ Blue whales (*right*) and minke whales (*above*) were killed in such large numbers that there were almost none left in the Antarctic oceans. This changed in 1994 when Antarctica became a whale sanctuary.

This modern Japanese whaling ship operates in Antarctica. Japan still kills whales in Antarctica for scientific purposes.

A Whale Sanctuary

In 1982, the IWC adopted the **United Nations** call for a 10-year **moratorium** on commercial whaling in Antarctica.

In 1992, Norway and Iceland tried, without success, to have the moratorium lifted.

Finally in 1994, with the urging of France and Australia, the IWC declared Antarctica a whale sanctuary. This means that whales in the oceans surrounding Antarctica are protected and cannot be hunted commercially.

Conservation of Antarctic Fish

In the 1960s, many countries extended their territorial waters to 200 miles (320 kilometers) off their coasts. Some of these new territories were now in Antarctic waters. This meant that many of the world's ocean fishing fleets came to the remote fishing grounds of Antarctica. Antarctic fish soon became threatened by exploitation.

As each species was exploited, the numbers of fish caught by the fishing ships dropped. This only encouraged the fishing companies to fish for another species, until its numbers also decreased.

▲▼ Antarctic cod (*above*), ice fish (*below*), and tooth fish have all been **overfished** in the past. Today, fish catches are controlled so that fish numbers do not drop below a certain level.

Conservation of Krill

Krill are tiny **crustaceans** that look like shrimp. They are found in huge swarms which cover hundreds of square miles of the oceans surrounding Antarctica.

▶ Krill are a key part of the Antarctic food web and need to be protected so that other fish and animals can survive.

Krill are the most **abundant** animal in the world and are a vital link in the Antarctic **ecosystem**. They provide food for many different kinds of animals, including fish, seals, whales, penguins, and other birds. They are a key part of the Antarctic food web.

World fisheries realized the value of krill as a great source of protein. In the 1980s, huge catches of krill were being taken. This human harvest of krill affected the many fish and other animals that depended on it for food.

In 1982, the *Convention for the Conservation of Antarctic Marine Living Resources* (CCAMLR) came into effect to protect and regulate the harvesting of krill, fish, squids, and birds.

The *CCAMLR* sets a limit on the numbers of fish and krill that can be caught, so that enough are left in the ocean. It also puts bans on catching particular species and sets up fishing zones to protect endangered fish.

The Madrid Protocol

A protocol is an agreement between parties (nations) that is signed by all the nations involved with it. The Madrid Protocol on Environment Protection was signed by the Antarctic Treaty consultative members in 1991. It has a detailed list of requirements that help to work out the impact that human activities have on Antarctica.

The Madrid Protocol says that Antarctica is a natural reserve devoted to peace and science. It also bans any mineral activity and mining, except for research.

The protocol also supports the conservation of plants and animals. Finally, it sets new standards for waste disposal and management, as well as the prevention of marine pollution.

▼ Oil spills are potentially a great environmental disaster for Antarctica.

▲ This Antarctic fur seal has been caught in a fishing net. The Madrid Protocol sets new standards for the prevention of marine pollution, which will help to reduce the number of animals harmed by waste and garbage in their environment.

❯ The Madrid Protocol sets strict standards for the removal of all waste from the Antarctic continent. This huge pile of garbage has been squashed flat and is ready to be shipped to the United States for recycling.

Huskies

Huskies, or sled dogs, are known for their strength and endurance. Teams of huskies were used in Antarctic exploration for nearly a hundred years.

▲ Huskies played an important part in most of the early Antarctic expeditions by pulling sleds filled with supplies and equipment.

In the 1960s, dog teams were combined with motor vehicles to survey and explore Antarctica.

Huskies were sometimes used for survey work of penguin **colonies** on the sea ice. However, after the 1970s they were used mainly for recreation. Today they have been replaced by motor vehicles.

In the early 1990s, huskies were removed from Antarctica because of concern that the dogs were damaging the environment and disturbing the wildlife.

◄ The last huskies left Antarctica in 1993.

The Antarctic Atmosphere

The Antarctic provides opportunities for scientists to study the atmosphere. Scientists hope to use the information to solve problems in Earth's atmosphere.

Scientists measure ozone levels in the Antarctic atmosphere.

The Ozone Layer

Ozone is a gas in Earth's atmosphere. It protects Earth by absorbing harmful ultraviolet radiation from the sun. Pollution and **CFCs** have begun to destroy the ozone layer. This has exposed Earth to more of the sun's rays, which is a serious worldwide problem.

The Greenhouse Effect

The atmosphere around Earth traps the sun's heat and warms the planet. Pollution in the air traps extra heat and makes Earth warmer than it would be naturally.

This climate change, called the greenhouse effect, is a major concern for the world. The warmer atmosphere may result in the melting of Antarctic ice. This would cause sea levels to rise, creating problems for many coastal countries.

Tourism

Antarctica fascinates many people because of its scenery, remote location, and wildlife.

Organized tourism began in Antarctica in the 1950s. Many tourists have visited Antarctica and the numbers will continue to grow in the future. The challenge is to find a balance where tourists can enjoy Antarctica without harming it.

▲ It is important that tourism is managed well to safeguard animal communities.

◄ Ocean liners transport tourists through Antarctica's spectacular scenery.

A Trip around Antarctica

In the summer of 1996–97, a ship with tourists traveled all the way around (circumnavigated) Antarctica.

Ship-based Tourism

Ship-based tourism causes little damage to the environment. Liners leave from Argentina, Australia, and New Zealand and usually visit the Antarctic Peninsula. Tourists only travel ashore for very short periods.

Fly-overs

Tourists fly over Antarctica in jet airliners. They can enjoy Antarctica's landscapes without harming the environment. However, some people argue that noise pollution from the airliners should be a source of concern.

The Impact of Tourists

If tourism is managed with strict environmental controls, it should be able to operate well in the future.

Many people will return home to promote the conservation of Antarctica as a continent of peace.

Tourism and the Madrid Protocol

The Madrid Protocol gives priority to science, but recognizes tourism as a use of Antarctic resources.

Tourists bathe in the warm pools of water on Deception Island, an active volcano near the Antarctic continent.

Scientific Cooperation in Antarctica

The value of Antarctica as a living science laboratory is now recognized around the world.

Under the Antarctic Treaty, scientists from different nations cooperate with each other and coordinate their research. This collaborative effort achieves far more than each nation working on its own. The remote position and the difficulty of working in such a hostile environment makes research very expensive. Working cooperatively can be more economical.

▼ This Russian–Australian scientific team works in Antarctica. People from different nations often work at one another's research stations.

► *Polar Duke* has laboratories, winches, and instruments that enable scientists to do research at sea.

Joint Cooperation

Nations that are better equipped willingly offer **icebreakers** and aircraft to help ships in difficulty or during medical emergencies.

▲ *Nathaniel B. Palmer* is a research icebreaker specially built for the Antarctic. It began operating in 1992.

Expeditions in the Field

Expeditions in the field may take four to six months, covering vast areas of snow and ice. The teams travel at 4 to 5 miles (6 to 8 kilometers) per hour over long distances. Tracked bulldozers pull trains of vans on sleds, which contain generators for heating and power for research. Other vans are for fuel, food, equipment, and housing.

Glaciology

Glaciology is the study of snow and ice. Scientists drill in the ice and take deep **cores** of ice from the **ice cap**. By studying the layers of ice built up over millions of years, scientists can find out about the climate in the past and, from that, make **predictions** about how it might change in the future.

▼ A tractor train transports a field hut over the icy ground.

⌃ A meteorologist measures wind speed at one of France's scientific stations on Antarctica.

Bar Codes

In order to conserve the Antarctic wildlife, scientists must understand how the ecosystem works.

Bar coding is used to study the **migration** of individual penguins. Bar codes, similar to those used at supermarket checkouts, are glued to the beaks of penguins. Scientists will record where the birds are found in the future.

Meteorology

Antarctica, with its huge areas of snow and ice, plays an important role in **global** weather patterns. Meteorologists use Antarctica as a scientific laboratory for measuring the extent and effect of global climate change. This is important to assess the greenhouse effect and changes in the thickness of the ozone layer.

Marine Biology

Marine biologists cut holes in the ice so they can collect samples of fish. The biologists study the fish to learn how they adapt to extreme cold.

⌃ The marine biologists who go into the Antarctic water to study marine life must wear special diving suits to protect their bodies from the cold.

Scientific Bases and the Environment

Most scientific bases are located on the 2 percent of the continent that is ice-free rock. The construction of buildings and the transportation and storage of fuel, combined with the activities of humans on the bases, all affect the native plants and wildlife in the environment.

Careful management of scientific bases is very important for the conservation and protection of Antarctica in the future.

Antarctic Garbage

Piles of garbage can be a danger to some of the wildlife around the base sites. Small pieces of plastic have been found in some dead birds at these waste dumps.

◀ Many forms of waste are produced on Antarctica. Much of the waste is removed from Antarctica and disposed of in the country from which it came.

Garbage in Antarctica

Typical garbage at base sites includes oil drums, **discarded** machinery, and plastic. Garbage like this could remain **intact** for years. The extreme cold and dryness in Antarctica prevents the quick breakdown of garbage.

▶ Empty fuel drums form a large part of the garbage on Antarctic bases.

Antarctica – A World Park?

Conservation organizations such as Greenpeace have suggested that the best future **option** for Antarctica is to make it a world park and list it as a world heritage site.

As a world park, the wilderness of Antarctica would have complete protection, although limited fishing might be allowed.

Antarctica would remain a zone of limited scientific activity, with cooperation and coordination among scientists of all nations.

Perhaps most importantly, Antarctica would remain a zone of peace, free of all weapons, and an important region for all nations of the world.

▶ The survival of many Antarctic animals may depend on what happens to Antarctica in the future.

Antarctic Fact File

The Land
Antarctica is a huge, frozen continent surrounding the South Pole. It has an area of 5.5 million square miles (14.25 million square kilometers) and is the fifth largest continent.

People
No **indigenous** humans have ever lived in Antarctica. Today, scientists, support workers, and visitors stay in Antarctica for varying lengths of time.

Animals
No native land mammals live permanently in Antarctica. Seals, whales, and penguins all inhabit the waters around Antarctica. Other seabirds live in and visit Antarctica.

The largest animal that lives permanently in Antarctica is a midge, a kind of wingless fly no more than one-half inch (12 millimeters) long.

Plants
Antarctica has no trees or bushes. Only two kinds of flowering plants, and simple plants such as mosses and lichens, can grow in Antarctica.

Coldest Place on Earth
Antarctica is the coldest place on Earth. The lowest temperature ever recorded was minus 129.3 degrees Fahrenheit (minus 89.6 degrees Celsius) at the Russian base, Vostok, in July 1983.

Antarctica's annual average temperature is minus 58 degrees Fahrenheit (minus 50 degrees Celsius).

Windiest Place on Earth
Winds have been recorded at 200 miles (320 kilometers) per hour at Commonwealth Bay.

Driest Place on Earth
Precipitation, which falls mainly as snow, equals less than 5 inches (12.5 centimeters) of rain per year. This makes Antarctica a frozen desert.

Highest Continent on Earth
Antarctica is the highest of all continents. Its average **elevation** is 7,546 feet (2,300 meters) above sea level.

Highest Mountain
Antarctica's highest mountain is Vinson Massif in the Ellsworth Mountain Range. It is 16,860 feet (5,139 meters) above sea level.

The Antarctic Ice Cap
The Antarctic ice cap is a thick sheet of ice which covers almost all of the continent. At its deepest, the ice is more than 14,700 feet (4,500 meters) thick.

Antarctica holds 70 percent of the world's fresh water in the form of ice.

Ross Ice Shelf
The Ross Ice Shelf is a huge, floating cliff of ice 30 to 45 miles (50 to 70 kilometers) above sea level. Along the coast, pieces break off the ice shelf and form icebergs.

Glossary

abundant   a great quantity or huge number of something

Antarctic Circle   an imaginary line around the South Pole at about 66.5 degrees south latitude

CFCs   harmful chemicals that were once used in refrigerators, spray cans, and packaging

claim   to assert ownership of land or property

colony   a group of the same type of animal living together

conserve   to keep something just as it is

core   a section that is shaped like a thin, solid tube

crustacean   an animal like a crab or shrimp which has a hard outer covering

discard   to throw away

ecology   the relationship between an animal and its environment

ecosystem   a community of living things

elevation   height

endure   to cope with something that is difficult

exploitation   to abuse or destroy something

extinction   the point where a type of animal completely disappears

geomagnetism   the study of Earth's magnetism

global   relating to the whole world

icebreaker   a strong ship which is able to break through ice

ice cap   the huge covering of ice over Antarctica

indigenous   having always lived in a certain place

intact   in one piece

isolation   being cut off from everyone else

meteorology   the study of weather and the atmosphere

migration   the regular travel from one area to another

moratorium   a temporary ban

myth   an imaginary thing

oceanography   the study of the oceans

option   choice

overfishing   endangering a type of fish by catching too many of them

precipitation   moisture that falls from the sky to Earth

prediction   a guess based on available information

ration   a small amount of food

regulate   to control

remote   a long way from anything else

resume   to begin again

South Pole   the southernmost end of Earth

species   a type of animal

stake   to lay claim to land

sub-Antarctic island   an island that lies in the warmer waters that surround Antarctica

suspend   to stop something for a certain amount of time

territorial   relating to the ownership or control of an area of land or water

United Nations   an international organization that tries to maintain world peace and cooperation

Index